# A Life

# IAIN CRICHTON SMITH

## *A Life*

Carcanet

First published in 1986 by
Carcanet Press Limited
208-212 Corn Exchange Buildings
Manchester M4 3BQ
108 East 31st Street
New York, NY 10016 USA

**British Library Cataloguing in Publication Data**
Smith, Iain Crichton
A Life.
I. Title
821'.914     PR6005.R58

ISBN 0-85635-644-1

The Publisher acknowledges financial assistance
from the Arts Council of Great Britain

Typeset by Bryan Williamson, Swinton, Berwickshire
Printed in England by SRP Ltd., Exeter

# Contents

*Lewis*
1928-45

## 1.

'When did you come home? When are you leaving?'
'No I don't...don't think I know...'
The moonlit autumn nights of long ago,
the heavy thump of feet at their late dancing.
'We'll sail by the autumn moon to Lewis home.'
'I think I know you...' But our faces age,
our knuckles redden and webbed lines engage
eyes that were once so brilliant and blue.
The sharp salt teaches us. These houses, new
and big with grants and loans, replace the old
thatched walls that straggled in a tall lush field.
I lie among the daisies and look up
into a tall blue sky where lost larks chirp.
The sea is blazing with a bitter flame.
'When are you leaving? When did you come home?'
The island is the anvil where was made
the puritanical heart. The daisies foam
out of the summer grass. The rigid dead
sleep by the Braighe, tomb on separate tomb.


## 2.

All day she sleeps but often in the night
she calls on her dead mother, her live son.
Her pills and bottles shine in the harvest moon.
She who was once beautiful hangs on
to her frayed thread of being: will not die.
She speaks in two languages in the night,
will dance like a light cloud, as once she did
with the luminous others at the corner of the road.
The stunning moon is cruising overhead,
the stacks of corn are gossiping in the field.
There was a time when she would starve for bread.
'Mother' she cries, 'mother' and that shield
of cloth bends over her. My child, my child.
She runs home lightly to her thousand pills,

9

her clouded marbles. And the daffodils
spring upward once again behind her heels.
The hills are cardboard blue, the skies are red.


3.

Our landmark is the island, complex thing.
A rock, a death, a house in which were made
our narrow global seaward-going wings,
the rings of blue, the cloth both fine and frayed.
It sails within us, as one poet said,
its empty shelves are resonant. A scant
religion drives us to our vague tremens.
We drag it at our heels, as iron chains.
A winsome boyhood among glens and bens
casts, later, double images and shades.
And ceilidhs in the cities are the lens
through which we see ourselves, unmade, remade,
by music and by grief. The island sails
within us and around us. Startled we
see it in Glasgow, hulk of the humming dead,
and of the girls in cornfields disarrayed.


4.

You will not find a Rubens, Rembrandt here,
nor my revered Vermeer. You will not find
the velvet-lined
hound faces of aristocrats: the blind
blank mask of genius with its gravid stare.

The meagre furniture appals me here,
the props of rock, of heather, and of sea,
the constancy
of ruined walls and nettles. A humming bee
is smartly burning round an absent pier.

Life without art, the minimum. I hear
a sermon tolling, for your theatre is
the fire of grace,
hypothesis of hell, a judging face
looming from storm towards boats and sea-drenched gear,

the thrifty fields, monotonous, austere,
where poppies are superfluous, and the rose.
The thistle grows
its thorny purple crown: and Sunday flows
with its burning transient girls through psalm and prayer.


5.

Once famous footballer, he's alcoholic now.
He'll speak to no one, crying through bare rooms.
O what has happened to that fragrant bough?

Shin-guarded and striped-stockinged, he ran out
to fields of local shadow and of sun,
was wasp in quickness and in freshness trout.

And poked the girls at night among the stacks
in his horned majesty: the moon a clear
ball that was spinning through vast cloths and racks,

discarded knickers. O spread legs of white.
He staggers past the mirror in his room
and dribbles helplessly. His early strut

on studs descends to shuffle. In this globe
the sunny whisky burns. The shadows ray
across him pitching towards his moony ebb.

He kicks right through the mirror. Is it day?
The spidery keeper hurts him in the rib.

6.

O hi ro O hi ree,
dance the reel beside the sea.

The wedding dances out three days.
The roads of moonlight are a blaze

across the strait. It starts again.
The red breeds red, the green breeds green.

The brilliant boxed melodeon
squeezes out a husky tune,

and legs are twined with legs, while one
sucks whisky with a baby's grin.

The red breeds red. It all begins.
The bridal gown's a wheel that spins

among the rocks. The river roars.
In darkness at the play of horse

he jockeys home. Triumphant sails
billow the firth above hard keels.


7.

In school it was, each morning, and her bum
divine and rounded. Mr Cicero Trill
burns on his pyre and hears its ceaseless hum
in sizzling Carthage while that ruined sail –
his cloak – hustles him Rome- and duty-wards. O love,
who but Catullus could inscribe those pains,
or exiled Ovid. At each window pane
the leaves are rustling. In carved white she sits
behind a desk that's scored beneath her tits.
Her bum is glorious, stern of the boat that rides

his tourist Mediterranean. So fresh and young.
The fire is flickering its viper tongue.
Virgil is burning with a wealth of brides.
The chalk trills crazily down her fleshy sides.


8.

Beside the library, I smelt the salt
as once I used to do,
the island boy with the *Tatler*, *London News*,

in their black leather covers. Shooting grouse
was not his special thing. Nor was the wine
red in his cup, nor the marbly and 'divine'

bare shoulders his. The snouting drifters drowsed
beside the pier. A sailor wove a net,
green among orange buoys. The hull was set

exactly on its shadow, and the gulls
were streaks of avarice. It was the drowned
slept neatly in their hammocks without sound

in the plain water among salty shelves.
The knickerbockered gentlemen expel
their smoky bubbles, and they come to heel,

the obedient beagles, then set out in line
into the crumbling sunset, and their haul
the dripping dead, so foxy-faced and tall.


9.

Remember how the War brought the News home,
John Snagge and Belfrage... The new wireless was
a huge mahogany. Each HMS

sunk in the Mediterranean might be ours.
Always 'the next of kin have been informed.'
I see them sheltering from the random showers

in seas they hadn't heard of, and the guns
defend the poor thatched roofs. In hollow booms
our HMS Accumulator runs

deep down to zero. In the box they see
young bodies hearsed. A vibrating Big Ben
tolls out their deaths, in the inconstancy

of an ocean named, unfathomable. They come
running from the playing fields which are blue.
They stutter out in classrooms words and sums.

That bitter water schools them through and through.


### 10.

Roses, I think there is salt on you,
and on the headland I hear the exiles' songs.

The thatched roofs, woven by dead hands,
are sunk among the superannuated school buses,

in a field of daisies and lush grasses.
The buzzard slants over the untilled ground.

Varying perfumes taunt me. In church I saw
the fifty-year-old girl I used to know,

her face curdled and gaunt. Bibles
are open in the churchyards, marbly white,

and the sea sighs towards the gravestones.
On the moors

14

the heather is wine-red and the lochs
teem with unhunted fish. The sky

is an eternal blue and God drowses
momently from his justice. Singing,

the drunk sways among poppies, missing
the rusty unused scythe. The boats are

a frieze on the far horizon, smoking gently,
and almost motionless. The cornfields were

a nest of snaky legs: and now it is
the butterfly that wafts there. This is not

a haunt of angels. The devils kneel at night
offering whisky in a bottle to

those who despise church windows in their reds.
Gaunt girl I walked with in the long ago,

sleep gently in the beams of the red moon,
whose claws are crablike in your drained breast.


11.

They get off the buses at the ends of roads,
walk the rest of the way. The vague butterflies

are wafting all around them. In the ditches
whisky bottles, empty lager cans.

The windows of the school are red shields,
the sky a waste of embers. Soon the stars

will begin to swim among oblique scents.
The spirits of sailors sigh along the walls

returning home at night from Canada,
where paunchy men with sky-blue suits and ties

flourish on memories of their Scottishness.
Slowly the moon rises like a ball

that was once a vague horn. You hear the moos
bring you home to your extended house

beside the old one which your grandfather
when still a boy signed with his careful name.


### 12.

Stubs of pipes in teeth, the old men
predicted good weather. It was our annual

visit to the town. Red apples
nested among their straws, as if birds

we did not know of hatched them. And the cones
were cold on icy teeth. Hardy, Laurel,

plunged out of windows on their rubbery ladders
in thin or baggy trousers. Errol Flynn

wearing smoked glasses had the Japanese
pilot in his sights. On Wake Island

we left the wakes behind, and strode, blinded,
into the brittle sunlight. This town is

too small for both of us, bowlered minister.
The colours of the cinema warmer than

your plain clear window. Till we reach our homes
we ride the gulches of these starved fields.

*Aberdeen University*
1945-49

The glitter of the water and the wake...
Heading for University in Aberdeen.
It's an autumn morning. I am seventeen.
Above the Isle of Skye the dawn's a flag

of red infuriate ore. I see the train
for the first time ever steaming from the Kyle
beyond the screaming seagulls, in the smell
of salt and herring. There's a tall sad crane.

The landscape, rich, harmonious, unwinds
its perfect symmetry: not the barren stone
and vague frail fences I have always known.
I hold my Homer steady in my hand.

All day we travel and at last dismount
at the busy station of that sparkling town.
A beggar with black glasses sitting down
on the hard stone holds out his cap. I count

the pennies in it. Should I freely give?
Or being more shameful than himself refrain?
His definite shadow is the day's black stain.
How in such open weakness learn to live?

I turn away, the money in my hand,
profusely sweating, in that granite blaze.
Unknown, unlooked at, I pick up my case.
Everything's glittering and transient.

2.

The prim historian talks of Robespierre.
Shakespeare's *Othello* is a mineral play
suited to granite and the wide North Sea.
Each subject has its scrupulous compere.

The guillotine cuts sharply between me
and that far island nesting in its waves.
Roof upon roof creates collapsing graves.
'Put up your bright swords.' Dewy Italy

and Aberdeen and Lewis all collide.
The sea-green incorruptible sustains
the sodden salty flesh. I shake my chains.
Europe is glowing like a flowery bride

with her fresh bouquets; and that ring recedes
mile upon mile away from me. I hear
the sharp quick yelp of tight-frocked Robespierre.
Some wound within me bleeds and bleeds and bleeds...


### 3.

'Youse students with the cash,' says Mrs Gray,
our iron landlady with the Roman nose.
(Her stuttering husband is a paler ray.)

What art, what music, troubled even once
her brow that's wrinkled by the thought of gold?
She fills the space around her, holds her stance

against the world's obliquity. She stakes
her confident site out, while the scholar ghosts
through a double landscape of new streets, old Greeks,

a sturdy lady not to be put upon
by tragedy engendered in the soul,
nor by her husband who drives buses down

familiar roads, and who at night attends
religiously the 'flicks', whose bedroom is
the moony attic that her greed commends.

## 4.

Beowulf dives into mysterious depths...
The girls on Union St in cruising pairs
clutch shiny handbags, and wear Woolworth rings.

He swarms in armour towards an old death.
In Hazelhead their legs are white and bare.
They swim in twilight wafting vague soft scents.

His bubbling armour frays and leaks and dents...
Their breasts at evening swell, their short skirts flare.
We are such fleshy fiery tenements.

The salty hero strides about his tents...
My dear pale girls with permed and lamplit hair...


## 5.

Bicycles sparkle past the market place.
The cafes glitter. Love O Careless Love.
The statues cast their shadows across parks.

The velvet-jacketed pensioned Major moves
a piece on the draughtsboard in the open air.
This is a mimic and yet serious war.

I lie in Duthie Park with the *Aeneid*,
in my white flannels. All the epitaphs shine
in the adjacent overgrown graveyard.

LOVE O CARELESS LOVE. The Odeon towers
in its white marble towards a blue decor.
Its transient images are what etch and burn.

And in the cafe a small radio plays.
Everything passes, everything is weighed
with a random music, heartbreakingly sweet.

6.

Aberdeen, I constantly invoke
your geometry of roses.

Your beads of salt
decorate my wrists

and are the tiny bells
of grammar schools.

There are no deaths
that I recall

among your cinemas,
in the shadows

of your green trees.
Aberdeen,

I loved your granite
your salt mica.

Your light
taught
me immortality.


7.

No library that I haven't loved.
My food is books.

The grey-haired twittering lady climbs the steps
to drag a heavy Spenser to the floor.

She is not made of crystal but is mortal.
An old professor is bent over a chair
drowsing perhaps sleeping.

How reconcile
the market to the library, the till
to strict Lucretius?

The foam of flowers in Duthie Park, the page
blazing in its whiteness, in this sun
whose sleepless socket is perpetual.

The grey-haired lady lugs a tome across
a library floor as polished as a glass.

O she will die but this book will never die.
The Faerie Queene; this pale dishevelled one.


*8.*

In winter, ice and frosty Aberdeen
inscribes its images on window panes.

The Polar star is miles away from us.
It glows on towers and ghostly lighthouses
and on the spiky Latin in my room.

This is your weather, strict Lucretius.
How can religion stand it? How can Pan
with his hairy tropic legs? That animal?

The frost an exhalation of the mind.
The icy planets keep their rectitude.
Religion dies in temperatures like these.

And God the spider shrinks in his crystal web.
The gravestones bloom with ice. The city is
a constant shrine of probabilities.

*National Service*
1950-52

## 1.

The corporal struts briskly up and down,
moustached, Hitlerian. 'You play fair with me
and I'll play fair with you. Otherwise…'
We stand at attention in the barrack room
beside our beds. There's a black ancient stove.
The sentry at the gate had glassy boots
and glassy eyes. The reapers in the fields
waved towards us as we trudged the dusty road
in the last hot July of our free youth.
We lay in our grave sheets as the Last Post
wailed through the room, a lost mysterious soul,
the bugle music of our homesickness.
The lights of our windows faded towards the square
where the RSM, a brutal cockerel,
had shouted as we trudged towards the door
which shut on Milton and on Shakespeare.


## 2.

'Listen, you poof, I'm standing on your hair.'
The public schoolboy smiles, superior
to this old patter. He's an officer
already in his mind, he will not fail.
The plumber's mate is shaking as his shots
miss the ringed target, small as a postage stamp.
His eyes are wells of weeping. The ball-cock
rises, a perfect circle, buoyant, light.
The public schoolboy registers a bull.
Last night he played some melancholy jazz
while we spat on boots and burned them luminous black.
The plumber's mate was reading *Dracula*.
The public schoolboy casually turned a page
of *Murder in the Cathedral*. The shots slam
into the distant circles. The red flags
swell in a breeze that's cool, civilian.

Education sergeants, lowest of the low...
Our NCO looks hunted, vigilant,
bearing fresh files wherever he will go.
We teach the recruits about NATO, UNO,
drowsy from ten mile marches. No one more
soldierly, crisply creased, than our NCO.
His badge is shiny, he's meticulous,
We teach letter-writing to the illiterate
easily unearthed, in spite of shame,
since they're the ones most charged. Unreadable,
Company Orders, but particular
their sense of personal honour, and their name...
The poster says, *Make the Army Your Korea.*
The burly RSM shadows the camp
red-cheeked and bulbous-eyed. We are the grit
of education sticking in his eye.
The haggard Wracs pass by in khaki skirts.
'I'll get that skiver Morrison,' he says
of our librarian. For BAOR
he pines at evening into his tearful glass.


4.

*Love O careless love. Irene, Good Night.*
The corporal actually talks to us, smokes our cigs
obsequiously donated. Brute mugs
often turn handsome as the gunfire fades.
Alone, the plumber's mate engilds his badge.
The Glasgow boys who masturbate at dawn
below gigantic sheets appraise their bints.
We are now bowed to these harsh elements.
The plumber's mate is exiled from his kind,
obsessed and jumpy. The omnivorous
witticisms tear him limb from limb.
The corporal approves, in sleepy calm:

our lotus land this squalid barrack room,
the harmless rifles stacked along the wall.


5.

We marched so beautifully, cleanly, then.
It was a perfect music wrought from pain.
EYES RIGHT – the general serenely shone

medalled and ribboned, a commissionaire.
The organ rose in blue... How strict and bare
the square at morning. Stony birds will share

its perfect stoniness. The reapers fade
into their corn and poppies. Sheared, I tread
this glorious echoing stage, exude

a rich fine scent of lotion.
                    It is done.
I enter the barrack room out of the bright sun.
It is a well of shadow. I lie down

extended on the bed, and see the blood
rolling along the floor. The head, the head...
The plumber's mate unrecognisably dead

but for the comic with its bleeding fangs.
The victim bubbles gently and the wings
turn ugly on the Quisling. A bee sings

thinly on a pane that's turning red.

*Clydebank and Dumbarton*
1952-55

## 1.

The adjective clause, the adverbial and the noun –
how would these boys consider them divine
as the bell-cheeked monks had done

in mediæval gardens? In pale neon
where tenements sag brokenly: or at noon
where they burn like cages; how could these girls shine

with laurel, not with lipstick? Random buses run.
How could that stairhead bowl be the carved urn
of shadowless Greece or Rome? Those pipes a vine

twisting and turning on that barren stone?
They're taught by what they are. That barbarous wine
boils over grammar and will not decline.


## 2.

Alliteration, simile. He composed
his yellow booklet when day's work was done.
Such careful bureaucratical fine prose!
Metonymy, synecdoche, the pun.
Over this grimy grid he superimposed
the texts of Greece, the scholars' monotone.
Beyond his window a cloud snottily flows.

A cage for bees and wasps! A lined fine school!
The chalk's a ghostly dust for such as these.
O somewhere else they find the beautiful,
the unpredictable flashes of girls' knees,
the curves of football that transcend all rule,
the poetry of the Clyde so silvery cool –
down sudden avenues green crowns of trees.

## 3.

The flash of trains on rails, the Cenotaph,
how shall these meet, collide?

Pale girls at evening on neon roads –
the marble halls of Rome.

Cloth-capped Glaswegians with their spotted hounds –
great Homer in his pride.

The vested hairy-chested boilerman
soaping his body in the kitchen sink –
the libraries and tomes.

And yet as legionaires they once set out
thump thump on knife-straight roads,

creating once their strong geometries
to link damp hut and hut.

## 4.

Seen here from green Argyll, the city is
a yellow labyrinth where each winking house
composed a bracelet of pure randomness.

The emptiness and hollows of the street!
The scholarly lamp-posts each with their viperish light
reading the stone. Each pack had its own suit

like grape flies gathered in the evening.
The sallow girls imagined a red ring
blazing on their fingers. The trains sang

and whined like wolves along predestined rails.
Among these garish ads the spirit fails.
The watery twilight of a million souls

composes jesters' colours. Where is home?
Not in this place with its tubercular bloom.
The city is a painted yellow room

for actors without denouement. I stand
inside the Underground. There's a hollow sound.
The whooshing train casts papers to the wind.

*Oban*
1955-82

## 1.

Oban in autumn, and reflective Mull
cast on the water. How the snowy gull

pecks at waste herring bones on the scaly quay.
The central glitter of the boundless sea.

Like pots that boil on Sundays, engines find
their drumming destination, and the mind

its fixed direction. By tall cliffs I see
the jackdaws playing. On green benches the

tourists repose at evening, while the tide
whispers and chuckles. O I see you, bride,

Gaelic, mysterious: and this radiance is
the extravagant presence of the sea's abyss

extending to Iona and its graves.
The very stones are green. The sea is sheaves

of endless blue on blue and lucid crowns
of jellyfish drift lazily. No one drowns

in this amazing light. The War Memorial burns.
One soldier helps another through the stone.


## 2.

A Roman rector, measured gravitas,
a Gaelic scholar too. He knows each child.
Our own names honour us and each one salutes

us from his sparkling bicycle. The school hums,
directed engine. Black-winged he comes
along the shiny corridors. In the hall

39

appointing prefects he quotes from Paul.
The race is to the kind, not to the smart,
to Brutus not to Antony. The clear art

of human Homer is our constant aim:
whatever's comely. Casually he says,
'It was Housman taught me in my Cambridge days.'

And behind him Macintyre and William Ross.
Where's Eliot and Auden? Horace glows,
each marble phrase, the clarity of prose.

'Transposing Greek to Gaelic is no toil.
They had their clans, their sea terms. And the style
of the great *Odyssey* is what Gaelic knows.'

Easily he chats to the crofting man
who sucks a straw: as easily as he scans
those vast hexameters or the pibroch.

                        Does
what's comely and what's right by natural rule,
by Roman cheerfulness and harmonious Greek.
Propounds a human yet a rigorous school.

3.

To find the way!
The raindrops glitter,
Lucretius's idea.

To let the light
sway through the marble –
temporal appetite.

To keep the mist
about the grammar
in the amethyst

bloom of violet.
Sheep's eyes
cast greeny jets

and grass waves –
itself how lightly
over graves.

4.

That sunny Gaelic world! That Roman rule!
Addison and Lamb. And Keats who died
in perpetual autumn with the nightingale.

To be centred in a place where the pure tide
renews its treasures: and each misty hill
is real yet poetic. There abide

the famous dead who walk the promenade
at watery evening when the world is still.
Around the moon the scholarly stars reside,

survive our light. I know the miracle
of the perfect bridegroom and the perfect bride
chiming exactly. Sometimes there's a style

we wear at moments, almost deified.
We see in others what ourselves compel,
inscriptions of our happiness. There's a wide

ocean, yet a margin of the will.
The prefecture and others. The divide
is what moans nightly as tides ebb and fill.

## 5.

Around the library
there is a cry,

unauthorised, casual.
They toil

to build the marble.
They scribble

their transient names.
Tattooed arms

scandalise the Forms.
In dreams

they're famous and see
in the huge screened smoky cinema

themselves enlarged. In beds
become immortal. O words

how stamp these wrists?
They pay for visits

to castles they themselves raised
in winds swayingly composed.

## 6.

Spinsterish teachers, missing the apples, die
quite abruptly, or in Homes
sleep beyond plasticine and nursery rhymes.

After retirement they venture
into Geography into History,
posters and labels of the day,

from the simply presented alphabet.
Their grey hair is combed white.
The wind and tenements confuse

with random uncorrected news,
scraps of jotters in the gutter,
homeless incorrigible litter.

I think in ashen corners they
suffer for their innocence,
the prim precision of their stance.

Their children swarm far afield.
Among projects they grow old.
None shall repeat his circumstance.


7.

Come towards me, immense millions.
From the carved desks I see you rise:
and you, ghostly inscribed blackboards,

be the red shield of a new sun.
I constantly see the stain
spreading on my calm jacket.

I constantly see the braid
unwind, unseam. The million dead
illuminate the million tides.

The feathered quill
is stained with red. The terrible
agonised cry infects the page.

Your helpless rage
shakes the tranquil gold board
on which the Duxes' names are scored.

## 8.

The unpredicted that I prize
blossoms in a furious
dishevelled spring.
        Around the lectern
the plebs, candle-white, arise.
Sir is shaken. His gown flows
along a suddenly turbid Styx.
The red marks on his rigid index  .
recall the blood of those who've died,
anonymously. The outraged dead
stand up in rows. The sparsely fed
gnaw at his prose and will not hide.


## 9.

Peasant that you are, realise
that you belong with them.
Your village is hideous

with the blood on the door
and your grass
is their grass.

It is the same wind
that blows everywhere,
and islands

howl with the same seas,
the white
foam on the lips.

It is the rigour,
exactitude, appals
without mercy,

and the homeless ones
rise on waters
unjustly flamed.

Peasant,
I order you
stand with them

when the epauletted one
ticks off on his register
their names.

Consider
that the loved chimneys
are for all of us,

and the castle
reflects the blood-red rays
of the diligent

whose epitaphs
are the torn washing hung out
on ropes themselves have made.


*10.*

'Please, sir, I don't read books...' she says to me.
Who on the Tiber Bridge were the famous three?

'Horatius, Stout and Lartius...' It is true
the fabulous Elvis with his *Blue Suede Shoes*

sways in their stony garden, *Paper Roses*.
At intervals they comb each other's tresses

with sleepy tenderness. 'I'll be a pilot, sir,'
says one to whom all writing is a blur,

'an engineer, an architect.' The girls yearn
for glamorous hairdressing, where helmets burn

as if on space men. Through neglected terms
they dream of dances and of wavy perms.


### 11.

Sometimes in supermarkets at the till
I see them tapping. Sometimes in hotels
I see them serving – all these Annabels,
these Floras and Fionas! Such sweet skill!

They tolerate, I think, my puzzlement,
conspirators together in a world
where life has been partitioned: and the blood
thinned down to chalk. Somewhere I see my pent

bourgeois persona, individual,
thornily investigate the rose
which raggedly pushed through pale slabs of prose.
The human flesh and the reflective jewel

to be combined and unified! The fixed
and unpredictable to sing as one –
the pale-faced girl chained to the changing moon,
and Venus smiling from her marble text!


### 12.

The teachers are growing old,
their faces whiter,
their eyes disillusioned and sad.

How long ago it was
when they played on their pupils like violins,
and *Macbeth* was a green field.

How joyful they were in those days
well-scrubbed and youthful
just as rich as the clouds.

Now their faces are chalk white
and the blackboards are singing
with a graffito of sour thorns.

13.

There was a time
when they could read Tennyson
to docile classes,
when poems rhymed.

when clad in their gowns
they seemed to be masters
of a finally colonised globe.

Now there is hubbub.
They are the chancy
scouts of the frontiers
and the chiming pentameters
have forsaken them.

They are no longer bearers
of messages from Rome and Greece,
the police
of the poem.

Unprotected, knobbly-kneed,
they must learn to bleed
their own, not Caesar's blood.

And in the marketplace
listen to Antony's address
with bitter grief.

For the chalk is like scrawls of lighting
on the black board,
and the sacred and abhorred
real poem has a waspish sting.

### 14.

'Sir, we are the stupid ones,' they say.
The football on the field invents a plot,
random and unpredicted. Who has taught
the inner rhythms of this outward play?

The English master with the grey moustache
watches from the touchline. 'Fodder, these...
But after all they rescued Rome and Greece
for the lucid talkers who turned pale as ash.'

Bewildering gyrations! On the wing
they flash fresh plumage, and the goal appears.
A ghost with gloves protects their universe.
The net behind him is a complex thing.

O graduate from this to Tennyson!
You fail at fences which the others raise.
We are practitioners of choice ideas.
It is our turn to listen and to learn!

*Taynuilt*
1982-

## 1.

Alone with my old typewriter at last
astronomy of letters I aspire
beyond its teaching to make literature.
Away from ghostly chalk I stand aghast

in this cold marble cell which will forgive
only the best and truest. Truant boys
from breezy woods, I hear your careless noise.
It is not by negligence that I must live

though not forgetting human voices too
in my study of the vases and the stone.
Beyond the sane and steady monotone
I listen patiently and must pursue

what shines beyond the grasses and the shade.
The leaves are trembling past my window pane.
By some fixed justice everything is weighed.
The truant boys are harried by a chain

that exactly measures both the loss and gain.
The value of the vase is always paid.


## 2.

What have I done today?
Read some of Aubrey's
*Brief Lives*, walked to
the newspaper shop and saw
the tenant below
feeding his golden cat
on a raw
plateful of meat.

A vast crowd
of seagulls landed to feed
on the mouldy bread
set out for the tit and the wren.
My table
rose towards me like a ruby
containing white sheet after sheet.
Was it this way
that Beethoven wrote his music or Mozart
dealt with his perfect art?
Did Homer, say,
shepherd the clouds to his roof
or suddenly laugh
at a joke made by the stone or the wood?
Life, life,
you are not respectable,
you are the sudden glance
of frilly knickers,
the unrepeatable
ray on the untidy work table
a drunk man saying his prayers.

Or according to Aubrey
'the worthiest men have been
rocked in the meanest cradles.'

'I'll have an umbrella invention
to retard a ship in a storm'
or of the Marquess Hamilton
(a beheaded lover of carps)
'would bring his fish into England
in barrels from Scotland
but their noses all turned green
from gangrene
by bobbing against the tub.'

Who is this poor worm then
who stands among apples and wine?

### 3.
*For Donalda*

So I come home to you
as the one I didn't leave behind
as the quick diligent
drawer back of curtains,

lest the house should be seen
as too much slept in
when there is so much wind
among the sunlight:

so many rainbows
trembling among news
of the daft old glasses
twinkling together:

so many owls
sucking to their eyes
the moon-struck mice
in the leafy classroom,

and the world a skirt
turning a corner
altering pleat by pleat
its breezy sculpture.


### 4.

If everything is contingent
how can the poem
be made necessary?

Like the summer rose
exact and perfect
in a coronation of dew.

Some come to the jail
of the inevitable sonnet
by unique suffering

demanding to be heard,
the song of the bird
in a metre of new thorns.


5.

The joy of the author is beyond speech.
His characters come dancing back to him.
They sing in the morning in his happiness.

Like the morning stars they are innocent,
enigmatic, diamond-like, without denouement.
They have such hope, they shine among dewy roads.

The joy of an author is beyond speech.
God, what do you think of us? Do you regret us?
Have our journeyings been sufficient justification?

The devil walks about the country in green,
colour of nature, suave, impenetrable.
You had to allow him his own perfect will.

And therefore the complainings of Job were heard,
the head becoming ashen, the pride dying,
the fire fading behind the black grate.

Are you happy with us, supreme author,
as other authors are in the evening
who scrupulously dine with their imaginings?

Such joy, such joy! Do not recall us to You.
Let us go on our way rejoicing
down all the possible avenues we can take.

Life is a sublime gift, supreme one.
What can it be compared to? Nothing.
Your stars are like the words that burn on carbon.

Let us go justly to our just denouement.
All that we ask of you is consistency,
not the arbitrariness of the partial one.

Only that the axioms should generate
the correct justice. Only that the ending should be
a perfect rainbow sprung from genesis.


6.

Never trust the author, trust the tale.
Out of the autumn mist it swims out to us,
a strange exhalation from the past
which is the tale remembering itself.

It is an affair of crows and of trees,
of clouds which bloom round chimneys, and of skies
that wear at once the first and last embers.

The author is not important, the author dies.
The tale lives on. It is the long river
heard at deepest midnight, in the day,
with berries hanging over it, subsumed
in a sweet water that is not a mirror.

Set out, set out, on your bare autumn sail.


7.

I think you will die easily.
You have been a book reader all your life.

You will not fight the imagination.

There have been so many deaths, *denouements*,
resolutions of plots,

and marriages at the ends of books.
We are always told of them
especially in the empire of Victoria.

So your death will be like a marriage,
as a return of the lost boy
to the house where he originally belonged,

after he had been punished in an orphanage,
forced to climb sooty chimneys,
to put varnish on coffins.

You will die in a cloud of roses,
the pages quietly finished,
the last disentangling chapter

putting all the characters in their places,
the marriages and deaths blossoming
from the final arranged words.


8.

Your brain is a thorn
that starves for meaning
as the thin cactus
with its single red flower.

Headaches remind you
of the vast distance
between your pale hand
and what your hand touches.

Headaches are the fields
of the thriftless thistles,
the rose which rises coolly
in a hiatus of pain.


9.

Don Quixote, through appearances
you stubbornly ride, a fragile skeleton,
ideal of the perfect and the true.

Common sense beside you, carnal, limited.
'Tell me if you were knight would you pee –
if to enchantment you were truly captive?'

The rusty voice creaks out against the proverbs,
wisdom of ages. Book-compelled
you kill your library of fictional villains.

Madman, idealist. 'Is this helmet, jug?'
A vase may be the armour of the poet.
Creation abhors wisdom, common sense.

You'll always be there, Sancho, by the wayside.
But for the other one who fights coffins, windmills,
let him be bridal to us, a fresh breeze.


10.
*For George Campbell Hay (1915-84)*

The vulnerable ones die many deaths
but if they are poets they rise again.

Kintyre, your adopted home, will have fresh leaves
in double April of the sun and showers
even when you're dead in your honey-coloured coffin.

The Middle East where you learned about man,
his beggary, nobility, still shines
with oil and violence, and the noise of war
prolongs itself beyond Tobruk, Bizerta…

And your country, Scotland, still remains the same
passive and hollow, the imperious thistle
nodding above a black and empty grave.

The vulnerable ones are the most precious
if from the desert they bring back reports,
with shaking hand record their victories –
no generals more valuable than they.

From lost Culloden towards Africa.
The judge condemns the beggar and the thief
but you recall the glittering, generous
waters, and the trees that do not fade.

Sweet gentle spirit, proud and breakable,
the mast is shaken but the boat survives.
The constant lyric of the possible
obsesses, the brief eternal wind
that trembles among leaves, and is the soul…

The Sahara, saffron, inescapable,
does not wholly burn you, nor the stars,
scatter of sand make you indifferent…

For though we are sand we are diamond. The slim waist
of the vulnerable hour glass brings such tears
as in the morning of your joyousness
when Kintyre was no mirage but the will itself
upthrust in mountains, towering and green.

## 11.

'We authors,' she will say, who has written nothing
but a single poem in a local paper.

'We authors,' she will say, so carelessly,
as if she were saying, 'We doctors' or 'We lawyers.'

Are you listening, Tolstoy, do you hear her, Burns?
Such a clear day, such a small coffee cup,

the statues being folded into leaves.
'We authors,' she will say and the earth is churning,

a thunderstorm swallows her white coffee cup,
and the lightning seals her lips with a blue flame.


## 12.

The jet plane leaves a trail in the blue sky.
The trail I leave is far more tortuous,

hesitations and false starts and grief and pain.
That plane with one explosion's far from us

in another country, almost another time.
I rhyme and sing in the ambiguous

but straight as a ruler is the trail you leave,
ambitious pilot, and conspicuous.

And mine is invisible and quite tentative.
Shall others find it straight, to the blue grave?

## 13.

Poet, you arise from the dead.
Among stones your shroud is palpable
changed into web, hung in the fragile day.

Nothing ever dies and you do not.
Leaf upon leaf is deathless and becomes
new forests for the climbing hectic tribes.

Leaf upon leaf, first green then white then green.
Nothing abhors you. You abhor nothing.
Even the spit of snails your soul loves.

The spirit uncrushable and breakable.
You die in green and you arise in purple.
The hills of evening remember you.

Your hand is the script of millions, of the dumb.
In you they live. Through you their blood returns.
Away with statues and remembrances!

Consider rather the bread of the spirit
imperishable wine. The changing shadow
of April is the soul, shy and yet public,
the private and the general at play.


## 14.

Such joy that I have come home to
after all that measurement.

A redbreast cautiously stutters
towards the bread cast on the lawn,

the cherry tree
mistily in blossom:

the swallow teeters
tenuously on a twig:

the roses
unfurl themselves.

The vole
noses in the garden:

and at its pail
the calf nuzzles.

We are part of this world,
tremble on the same ladder,
our flesh is beguiled
to the same soil.

Those who have lived here long
walk among old stones
lightly: and the clouds
are not strangers.

See how at night the moon
anchors among branches.

The dog barks from winking lights.
The crofthouses
have their roots deep in the pasture,
the straws smell of this air.

Blackbird
with the bracelet of worms
in your beak,
weasel
with the squeak
of the rabbit.

There is no storm
scrawls more locally than here:
its slant lightning
and the tackety boots of the thunder
are known.

Under the stone
the worm is a slow train
unwinding its carriages.

The lark's beak flashes.
The lark spirals and sings.

## 15.

Latterly the sea would cast them up,
all your tragic heroes, doomed princes.
In their blue tunics they would all rise

with belts of green seaweed about them.
Better than statues were these human hands,
the eyes surprised by the luck of nature.

The earth that echoed with its antique armour
gave way to the various language of the sea,
its furious onsets, sunny promises,

its bony headlands softened by spring flowers,
its billowing robes, its briny theatre,
betrayals forgiven, sunk among iron keels.

## 16.

There is no island.
The sea unites us.
The salt is in our mouth.

I have heard the drowned sing
when the moonlight
casts a road across the waters,
fine and luminous,
and each house sways
in its autumn light.

'The moon that takes us home to Lewis.'
to the dancing
to the phantoms of evening
to the charmed wells.

The island, as our poet said,
is an iceberg.
We bear it with us,
our flawed jewel.

As the sun sets
over the mountains
I see the homeless ones
forever rowing.
Their peasant hats mushroom,
like foundering bouquets.

The wakes
are for everyone
and the large sun
glints on the excised names
of the exiles.

'No ebb tide ever came
without a full tide after it' –
precious ones
whose flesh is my own,

and who arise each day
to a new desert.

The island, my vase, knows you.
Your inscribed faces
burn out of the brine:
this is the sharp wine
that educates us.

As we change
so the island changes,
we are not estranged
by the salt billows.

'There is no ebb tide
without a full tide after it.'
The tall white bride
accepts the fresh waters.